SAINT FRANCIS OF ASSISI

CTS Children's Books

CONTENTS

The city of St Francis 3

A special name 4

Francis in prison 6

The knight of Christ 8

'Go and rebuild my house' 10

Our Lady poverty 12

The Portiuncola 14

The first followers 16

Love for creation 18

At Greccio & La Verna 20

Francis' song 22

Text by Silvia Vecchini
Illustrations by Antonio Vincenti
Translated by Simone Finaldi

Saint Francis of Assisi: Published 2009 by the Incorporated Catholic Truth Society, 40-46 Harleyford Road, London SE11 5AY. Tel: 020 7640 0042; Fax: 020 7640 0046; www.cts-online.org.uk. Copyright © 2009 The Incorporated Catholic Truth Society in this English-language edition.

ISBN: 978 1 86082 562 0   CTS Code CH 17

Translated from the original Italian Edition **San Francesco D'Assisi** - ISBN 88-87324-77-8, published by Il Pozzo di Giacobbe, Corso Vittorio Emanuele 32/34, 91100 Trapani (TP), Italy © 2006 Crispino di Girolamo.

THE CITY OF ST FRANCIS

Assisi, in Umbria, is known throughout the world as the city of peace, the city of St Francis. In the thirteenth century, a magnificent basilica was built there in his honour, an incredible work of art; it has paintings by Giotto and other famous artists too. Everything about Assisi seems to tell us the story of Francis, a story that has moved people for hundreds of years.

A SPECIAL NAME

At the end of the 1100s, in Assisi, there lived a rich merchant called Peter Bernardone and his wife Joanna. Peter often travelled abroad to buy special cloths and fabrics. In 1181 or 1182, during one of these journeys, while Peter was in France, Joanna gave birth to a boy she called John, after John the Baptist. When Peter came back from his travels, he decided to give his son a different name, one that was not normal at the time. Peter called the boy Francis.

Francis grew up in Assisi; he was clever and quickly learned how to be a cloth merchant like his father. Unlike Peter, he was not greedy and was happy to share what he had with others. His friends were the sons of other merchants and he spent his time with them: He loved music and poetry, giving banquets and parties, playing games and having fun. Francis was special and different like his name; he was very generous because he wanted to be liked, but also because he really cared about what other people needed. When he was a young man, he wanted to join the army of Assisi so prepared a fine suit of armour for himself. However, he heard of a noble knight who had no amour, Francis gave his armour to the knight so he could go to war.

FRANCIS IN PRISON

When Francis was 20 in 1202, Assisi was at war with the city of Perugia. Francis wanted to fight and defend his city. There was a bitter battle on the banks of the Tiber river and Assisi's army, made up of nobles, merchants and poorer people, was defeated by Perugia. Many lost their lives and Francis was among those taken prisoner. Perhaps because of his fine clothes, he was put in jail with the nobles from Assisi.

It was the start of a difficult time, without family, friends or freedom. During his year in prison, Francis thought hard about his life, he thought about his experience of battle and asked himself many questions. He did not, however, become sad like the other prisoners; he did his best to be kind to his friends. Francis did not yet know his mission but felt that God was asking him to begin a great adventure.

THE KNIGHT OF CHRIST

While in prison Francis became very ill. Once he was freed, he recovered from his illness but the life he used to live did not make him happy anymore. He still wanted to be a knight since it seemed to him that loyally serving a noble lord was the best way to spend his life but he wasn't sure how to do it. Francis offered himself to go to the South of Italy to join the Pope's army. He set out and

when he arrived at Spoleto he had a strange dream: A voice invited him to follow the real 'Lord and not a servant'. Francis understood that it was Jesus who was calling him, the King of kings, and that as well as being a solider, there were other ways of being courageous and generous.

As he returned to Assisi, Francis felt he needed to be alone, he was often thinking of Jesus and how he could serve him. While riding his horse near Assisi, Francis met a leper. He lived in a place outside the town where lepers were taken because the people of the town were afraid of catching their disease. Francis stopped his horse, why should he be afraid? He wanted to be a knight of Christ and he knew that Christ loves the poor and the needy. He got down from his horse, put a coin in the man's hand and without fear, hugged and kissed him. Now Francis knew that this was the real battle; to love others and forget about yourself.

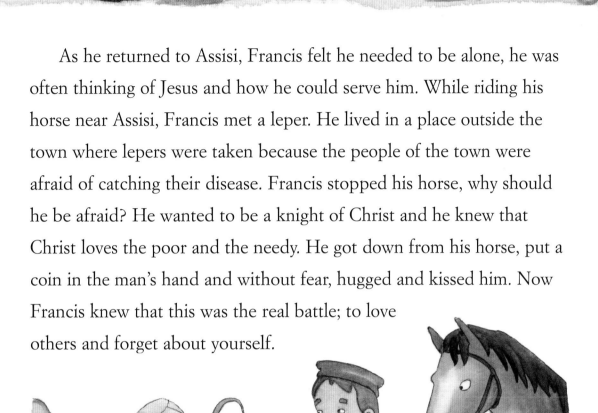

'GO AND REBUILD MY HOUSE'

Francis would go to the little Church of San Damiano every day, it was just outside the gates of Assisi. The walls were in ruins and the inside was bare, there was only an altar and a cross. Francis loved being in silence in front of Jesus on the cross, asking in his heart, 'Lord what do you want me to do?' One day while Francis was praying he heard a voice from the cross, 'Francis can't you see my house is falling down? Go and rebuild it.'

Francis was full of joy and wanted to do what Jesus had asked as soon as he could. So he began to work to repair the broken building. Everyone in Assisi made fun of him, he was supposed to be a great knight and now he had become a simple builder! Peter was angry because his son was making him look silly and using his money to rebuild a ruined Church that no one went to, but Francis carried on bravely.

Only later, would Francis understand that the voice on the cross was not asking him to repair a country Church but to renew the whole Church by his example of poverty and love.

OUR LADY POVERTY

Peter Bernardone, didn't know how to stop his son behaving so strangely, so he asked Guido the bishop of Assisi for help. Guido, who knew Francis and had seen how much he had changed, decided to talk to the father and son together. When they arrived, there were many people watching to see whose side the bishop would be on and if he could help bring peace to the family. Peter said that what Francis had done was wrong and the bishop said to the boy, 'Francis, your father is angry. If you want to follow Jesus give him back his money and don't be afraid. God will help you, you will have everything you need, even to rebuild your little Church of San Damiano.' Francis listened, then did something that surprised everyone: He began taking off his clothes and stood naked in the square wearing only a poor cloth. He put all his clothes and the money he was going to use for the building, in a pile and told everyone, 'From today, I want to follow

Christ and my only father will be God the father in heaven.' His father couldn't believe it and rushed away very angry, the bishop gave his cloak to Francis, who, having left his family and everything he owned, now belonged totally to God.

THE PORTIUNCOLA

Francis managed to get the stone and materials to repair the church of San Damiano, he lived on what people gave him and worked hard. When he finished, he went to another small abandoned Church called The Portiuncola. Francis fixed that one too.

While at Mass there one morning, Francis asked God what he should do now that the churches had been repaired. The priest read the Gospel in which Jesus sends out his disciples to announce the Good News, telling them:

'Take nothing for the journey, no staff or knapsack, no bread nor money, nor a spare tunic.' Francis was sure that Jesus had answered his prayer and given him an important mission to announce the gospel in poverty from village to village. So he left his sandals, bag and staff and wore only a rough tunic. From that day, Francis preached in squares and cities reminding people of God's love and forgiveness. He always began with the greeting, 'Pax et bonum' which means 'I wish you peace and all good', little by little, this became what all the people of Assisi say to each other.

THE FIRST FOLLOWERS

Francis encouraged people to change their lives and live in poverty and service, following Jesus and leaving everything else. Some of his listeners felt called to give their life for the gospel, like Francis. His first companions were called: Bernard, Peter and Leo and there were many others. Francis called these companions brothers or friars and he decided to go to Pope Innocent III to ask him to approve their way of life, based on poverty and living as Jesus had taught in the Gospels.

Arriving in Rome in 1210 they met the Pope, who said yes to their way of life and told them to cut their hair as a sign of leaving the world behind.

Meanwhile, in Assisi a young woman wanted to follow Francis' example. Her name was Claire and in 1212 she left her family and joined Francis, cutting her hair and putting on simple clothes like the rest of Francis' followers. Francis put a veil over her head and she took the vows of poverty, chastity and obedience. Claire would not be alone for long, and soon a second order was born, the 'Poor Claires'. Poor in the eyes of the world but princesses in the eyes of Jesus.

LOVE FOR CREATION

Why is Francis loved by so many people? Because even though he was poor and had nothing, he was happy and his happiness spread. He showed his joy in everything he did; while he worked, prayed, preached and helped people. Francis always blessed God. Francis was humble and wanted to be close to all men, even those no one else thinks about;  everyone who looked into his eyes felt loved. He loved even the smallest creatures... In his eyes even the smallest creatures were a sign of the love of God. One day Francis saw a field full of birds and leaving his brothers, he went to preach to them. The birds came down from the trees and stood still as if listening to him.

They didn't move even when some of his companions arrived. Only when Francis finished speaking and blessed them, did they fly away.

Another time, Francis went to Gubbio, where a fierce wolf had been frightening the people of the town. Francis decided to go and meet the scary beast and found him outside the city. While everyone was watching, he asked the wolf not to hurt the people anymore and in return they would give him all the food he needed. The wolf, who had become as quiet as a lamb in front of Francis, gave him one of his paws. Francis told the people that they should not fear hungry animals, but they should live without doing evil, forgiving each other and living in peace.

AT GRECCIO &
LA VERNA

Francis and his companions travelled a lot, all over Italy and even to Egypt and the Holy Land where Jesus was born and lived.

There were however, two very important places in Italy for his brothers. At a place called Greccio on Christmas night in 1223, Francis made the first Christmas crib. He recreated the scene of Jesus' birth, with an ox and a donkey.

They had a Mass and Francis read the Gospel of the birth of Christ. Then Francis brought a statue of the baby Jesus to put in the manger and something incredible happened: the people there saw a real baby moving and playing in Francis' arms.

In September 1224 he was travelling to a place called La Verna in the middle of a forest. One night while praying, Francis asked Jesus from his heart, to be even more united to him. There was a great light in the sky and Francis suddenly found that he had the same wounds that Jesus had on the cross and felt in his heart the immense love of Christ for everyone.

FRANCIS' SONG

The poor man of Assisi worked, prayed, fasted and helped people but he was not well; an illness was making him blind, he had bad stomach pains and was becoming weaker all the time. Francis however, never lost his joy and blessed God for everything. His brothers could see he was in difficulty and they brought him back to San Damiano and prepared a place for him. There he composes his Canticle of the Creatures, a beautiful hymn of praise to God for all his gifts.

Francis died in 1226.

After his death, the fruits of his simple but extraordinary life continued to grow, people loved him even more and his order took his message of peace everywhere. Francis immediately became one of the best loved saints in the world.

CANTICLE OF THE CREATURES

All praise be yours, Most High, all powerful, good Lord.
All glory, all honour and all blessing,
To you alone, Most High, do they belong,
No mortal lips are worthy to pronounce your Name.

All praise be yours, my Lord,
In all your creatures, especially Sir Brother Sun
Who brings the day; you give us light through him.
How beautiful he is, how radiant in his splendour!
He is the token of you, Most High.

All praise be yours, my Lord, for Sister Moon and the Stars;
You have made them in the heavens, bright and precious and fair.

All praise be yours, my Lord, for Brother Wind and the Air,
For every kind of weather, fair and stormy,
By which you nourish everything you have made.

All praise be yours, my Lord, for Sister Water;
So useful and lowly, so precious and pure.

All praise be yours, my Lord, for Brother Fire
By whom you brighten the night.
How beautiful he is, how merry, robust and strong!

All praise be yours, my Lord, for Sister Earth, our mother
Who feeds us, rules us and brings forth all manner of fruit
And coloured flowers and herbs.

All praise be yours, my Lord,
For those who forgive one another for love of you
And endure infirmity and tribulation.
Happy they who endure these things in peace
For they will be crowned by you, Most High.

All praise be you, my Lord,
For our Sister the Death of the Body,
From whom no man escapes.
Woe to him who dies in mortal sin.
Blessed are those who are found walking by Your most holy Will,
For the second death will have no power to harm them.

Saint Francis